ABOUT THE COVER: *In the summer the beautiful Bean Geese of Europe nest in the Scandinavian countries, often above the Arctic Circle. In the fall they fly south to spend the winter in central and southern parts of Europe.*

THE FRONT ENDSHEET: *A typical group of North Atlantic waterfowl as often seen just off shore in the migrating and winter seasons. Eiders are in background, Goldeneyes on the left, and Brants on the right.* THE BACK ENDSHEET: *Under the setting sun of the Australian dusk are seen Australian Shelducks in the foreground, Chestnut-breasted Teals at left, and Australian Shovellers at right.*

ACKNOWLEDGMENT: *Egyptian Tomb Painting. Thebes. p. 6. British Museum.*

DUCKS, GEESE, AND SWANS

BY BERTEL BRUUN

ILLUSTRATED BY LEIF RYDENG

THE ODYSSEY PRESS · NEW YORK

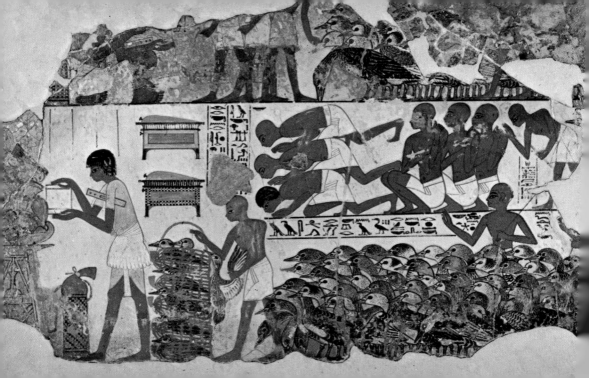

ON A December evening in the early 1800's, William Cullen Bryant tramped a road that wound through the Berkshire hills of Massachusetts, his mood a match for the gray weather. Then the last glow of sunset broke through the clouds, and a solitary bird traveled across the rosy sky. His spirits restored, Bryant went home and wrote *To a Waterfowl*. The young poet had learned a lesson: "He who, from zone to zone, / Guides through the boundless sky thy certain flight, / In the long way that I must tread alone, / Will lead my steps aright." ■ Bryant was

In this Egyptian wall painting (ca. 1500 B.C.) food grain is carefully measured out for domesticated ducks and geese. They were among man's most important sources of food.

far from the first man to find inspiration in waterfowl; from the earliest days of civilization men have been fascinated by ducks, geese, and swans. An ancient Egyptian wall painting of farmers tending their flocks suggests that the fascination is not entirely of the spirit; a roast bird makes a good dinner. And yet there is no denying men's delight in the vivid plumage of ducks, the grace of swans, the wild, free flight of geese, and these feathered creatures recur in the mythology, folklore, literature, and art of the world. ■ The Greeks believed Zeus made love to Leda in the guise of a swan. The Romans said the goddess Juno's pet geese cackled a warning when invaders moved secretly outside the city's walls. Denmark's Andersen gave us

the tale of the ugly duckling, and America's Disney the irate Donald Duck. Some American Indian tribes dance a duck dance. Legends of swan maidens are told in almost every land and have been borrowed by the ballet. ■ To this day, no British subject may own a swan without permission from the Crown; the famous swans on the Thames display "swanmarks," royal brands cut into their bills. ■ Ducks and geese were popular subjects in Chinese and Japanese art, and the swan a frequent motif in Empire furniture. Waterfowl have left a mark on everyday speech: *the goose hangs high, don't kill the goose that lays the golden eggs, duck soup, ducky, swan song.* Ben Jonson called Shakespeare "the sweet swan of Avon." And the philosopher Montaigne wrote: "Why may not a goose say thus: 'All the parts of the uni-

A single flock of Barnacle Geese may number many thousands.

9

verse I have an interest in: the earth serves me to walk upon, the sun to light me; the stars have their influence upon me; I have such an advantage by the winds and such by the waters; there is nothing that yon heavenly roof looks upon so favorably as me. I am the darling of Nature! Is it not man that keeps, lodges, and serves me?' " ■ Perhaps it is not surprising that ducks, geese, and swans have attracted so much attention; there are some 225 species scattered about the world. All belong to one large, diversified bird family called *Anatidae*, from the Latin, meaning duck. All are web-footed swimmers. Geese and swans are clad in rather somber colors of white, black, gray, or brown. It is the ducks that have the most brilliant plumage; furthermore, the male ducks—called drakes—

Trumpeter Swans, largest waterfowl, have 8½-foot wingspan. European Teals, among the smallest, have only a 22-inch wingspan.

Steller's Eider

European Widgeon

Mallard

King Eider

Shoveller

Ross's Goose

Bewick's Swan

Shelduck

Gadwall

White-winged coter

Black-bellied Tree Duck

One helpful key to the identification of the many hundreds of species and races of waterfowl lies in their characteristic wing markings. Ducks have a patch of color, called the speculum, on their wings.

are generally more colorful than the females. ■ In summer, however, after breeding is over, drakes of most species gather in flocks away from the females and shed all of their plumage including their flight feathers. They then grow the so-called eclipse plumage, which is, in its lack of colorful markings, almost identical to that of the females' plumage. Toward summer's end they begin to grow back their flight feathers and regain their brilliant, male markings. Many ornithologists believe their temporary loss of conspicuous plumage is a safeguard that makes them less visible to hawks and other predators during the flightless period. ■ Until recently, it was thought that

Ducks show great sex differences whereas geese and swans show little or none. Shown are 1. Baikal Teal 2. Hooded Merganser 3. African Pygmy Goose 4. Paradise Duck 5. Freckled Duck 6. White-fronted Goose 7. Mute Swan.

Falkland Flightless Steamers are the only ducks that can't fly. However they use their wings to "swim."

waterfowl depended wholly on an oily fluid for waterproofing their feathers. Ducks, geese, and swans do have an oil gland at the root of the tail. The birds press out a greasy substance with their bills, using it to dress their feathers when they preen. But the feathers themselves —their texture, and the way they overlap—plus a thick mat of down beneath the feathers, also help to keep the bird dry. ■ Ducks and geese are much alike in their manner of flocking and migrating. Single families, including three or four generations, may make small flocks within the breeding area. But when the

Fatty tissues help to keep ducks from freezing.

Interlocking parts of a feather help to shed water.

13

Waterfowl migrate in formations characteristic of their species. Brants (left) fly in long, wavering columns, while Eiders (right) fly in small flocks in short, straight lines.

time comes for migratory flight, the groups often merge until a flock of 150,000 or more birds fills the sky. A flock of swans, on the other hand, rarely numbers more than 500 birds. ■ The larger waterfowl, such as the Barnacle Goose and the American Brant, fly as fast as 50 miles per hour when migrating. The Whistling Swan can do 55. Although most ducks fly at a lower rate of speed, one of the swiftest of all the waterfowl is the Canvasback duck, which has been clocked at 70 miles per hour. ■ Cruising along the coast, waterfowl usually fly only a few feet above the waves. Inland, they usually remain below the clouds, but they often reach altitudes of 3,000 to 8,000 feet. The record for altitude is held by a flock of Bar-

Flocks of the migrating Canada Goose (left) made famous the familiar stream-lined V-formation while European Widgeons (right) fly in a "cloud" pattern.

headed Geese which was observed flying over a Himalayan peak about 20,000 feet above sea level. ■ On short hops, waterfowl generally fly in irregular formations; it is on longer migratory journeys that some species fly in characteristic patterns. Best known, of course, is the wedge, or V, used by flocks of Canadian geese, a formation which enables them to overcome the resistance of the air more easily. The lead bird, however, must break through the wall of air, and during a long flight a number of the geese in the flock will move up and take a turn at the rigorous task. Most waterfowl will use the wedge formation at one time or another in their migratory flights, but other formations are more characteristic. The American Brant, the Barnacle Goose, and the Blue Goose fly in long, undulating lines and wavering columns. Swans sometimes form long files of 400 to 500 birds. American Eiders fly just above the water in short lines, often following the indentations of the shoreline. Many species of duck, such as the Baldpate, employ a "cloud" formation.

■ Waterfowl follow long-established routes called flyways in their migrations. "The old ganders know the way," wrote the naturalist Arthur Bent, "and lead their trustful flocks, with the earth spread out below them like a map." The paths of various species may overlap or coincide for long distances between northern breeding grounds and southerly winter havens. Over North America there are four

Along the shores of western Europe are, from left to right, European Teal, Shovellers, Widgeon, and Bean Geese.

Before take-off Whooper Swans run across the water into the wind and use feet and wings as brakes when landing.

important flyways—the Atlantic, Mississippi, Central, and Pacific—and during spring and fall, each is a busy highway. ■ In the flyways of the western hemisphere, migrating wild swans are seen less frequently than geese and ducks simply because there are fewer of them, yet flocks of these one-time natives of Asia still make their way along the Atlantic and Central flyways. Migrating swans usually travel in small wedge formations, but a long line of more than 500 Whistling Swans has been observed flying south over the Atlantic shoreline at a height of less than 600 feet. Whistling Swans are a beautiful wild species of North

Mating displays are poses by which males attract females of their species. Most are confined to positions on the water or ground, but Old Squaws can perform them in flight.

America, and when in flight they utter a series of whoops, clucks, repeated *hoo-hoo's*, and soft trumpetings that resemble the cry of the Trumpeter Swan. Migrating swans are easily identifiable, for they fly with their long necks outstretched, and often with their black feet extended beyond their tails. ■ Because of their size, swans must take off facing into the wind. They first trip along the surface of water for 15 or 20 feet, flapping their wings as they beat the water with their feet. They then mount the breeze, and, once airborne, they move more swiftly with their slow, deliberate wingbeats than geese or any but speediest ducks. ■ Perhaps the most fascinating phenomenon of waterfowl behavior is that known as "display," which occurs during courtship. The males of most species perform rituals and show off their handsome plumage to the females. The swans are among the most graceful of birds during their mating displays. Two or three Whistling Swan males, or cobs, will parade with prancing steps before a female, or pen. With necks arched and wings spread wide, the rival cobs bow to the pen in an attempt to win her favor. Mute Swan cobs display in the water, dipping their heads into the water again and again, then gently reaching toward the pen with down-turned bills. ■ The courtship of geese is more aggressive. Audubon wrote that "a gander does not strut before his love with the pomposity of a turkey or the grace of a dove. I can imagine one who has just accomplished the defeat of

Mute Swans, by many accounts, are rather ill-tempered. Males, or cobs, are jealous guardians of mates and territory. In a threatening mood, they curve necks drastically.

20

Falcated Teal

Wood Duck

Mandarin Duck

Red-breasted Merganser

Steller's Eider

Harlequin
Duck

Ruddy
Duck

another male after a struggle of half an hour. He advances toward the object of contention, his head raised scarcely an inch above the ground. He hisses loudly, while the emotion which he experiences causes his quills to shake." ■ In most species of ducks, the females come into season irregularly during the breeding period. During the late spring, therefore, many drakes vie with one another in displaying for those few females in their species ready to pair at any given time. For this purpose,

Courting drakes have two important tasks. They must display their distinctive and chromatic species markings in such a way as to catch the attention of females of their own species, sometimes in marshes that are crowded with species of nearly like appearances. And they must also triumph over other drakes of their own species, if they are to win a mate. For this double job, each drake employs a display posture and behavior shared by the other drakes in its species.

23

Mallards

Common Goldeneyes

Gray-lag Geese

each species has developed highly ritualized display behavior. Among the Old Squaws, or Long-tailed Ducks, for example, the drakes congregate on the water in a circle around a receptive female, their tails erect and necks upraised as if for a formal ballet. ■ Each species of duck has its own way of display. The Steller's Eider drake pushes upright on the water to reveal its brown breast. Ruddy Ducks bend their tails forward, disclosing normally hidden white feathers. The gorgeous Wood Duck often perches on a branch above the water, where it need do no more than swell its throat to give the females a full view of its silken breast. Red-breasted Mergansers tip into the water, submerging the breast, and emit a mating call. ■ Mallards swim restlessly about in a group near a female. Each drake occasionally dips its bill into the water and makes a loud splash by snapping back its head. Rearing up on the

Courtships are conducted by means of a broad range of display behavior. Generally, a group of drakes congregates near any female ready to mate; she observes their antics and makes a choice. Mallards and Goldeneyes are among those suitors known for robust bowing and quacking. Ganders fight. Pintails (right) are perhaps the shyest of ducks, posing gracefully, and "mewing."

water, the drakes may make deep bows to the female, which sooner or later will swim to one of them and return the bow, indicating the successful suitor. ■ In the wild state, most ducks are polygamous, but cobs and ganders usually remain monogamous once they have won their mates. A pair will migrate together and breed each new season, going back to the old, familiar nesting sites year after year until parted by death. Domesticated geese and swans experience no such marital bliss; like the ducks, they are polygamous. ■ Unlike ganders and cobs, drakes seem to play a specialized role in the life of the species. The period of display and mating

Old Squaws are noted for an elaborate form of group courtship called "social display." Drakes surround a female, stiffen their tails, and swim in a circular fashion around her. These males are in summer plumage; the Old Squaw males in the picture on page 19 are in winter plumage.

is the high point of their annual cycle. After fertilizing their mates, they retire for the rest of the summer and during that time molt all of their feathers. They give little or no aid to the females during the period of nesting, incubation, and rearing of the young. ■ Ornithologists are not sure whether certain kinds of nesting behavior are instinctive or taught by parents to each new generation. Instinctively or not, the females of waterfowl use their own down, plucked from the breast, to line the nest insulating and camouflaging the eggs during the incubation period. ■ Europe's eiderdown industry provides artificial, sheltered nesting areas for Eiders, and down is harvested from the nests two or three times a season. Eider females replace the stolen down until they have plucked their breasts bare, after which they may substitute sticks and leaves as insulation for their eggs.

■ Waterfowl have become adapted to nesting in different types of terrain of their breeding grounds, not only for protection against predators, but also to ensure themselves sufficient space to nest in spite of competition. In Greenland, for instance, the Pink-footed Geese nest high on the ledges of cliffs. Here the geese are safe from one of their predators, the arctic foxes. While his mate is incubating the eggs, the gander stands watch nearby and will attempt to defend her against enemies. Many waterfowl, including most geese, nest in arctic regions. Here on the tundra, uninhabited by men, there is ample room and food for many nesting birds during the brief summer period.
■ In more common breeding areas, such as the

Eider female lines nest with down. By careful harvesting of such fluffy nests in Eider colonies, in Iceland and Europe, man developed a multimillion-dollar industry.

shores of northern lakes, where many species crowd the available grounds, geese have been known to take to the tall trees to nest. Shelducks sometimes move into rabbit holes or even abondoned fox holes to incubate their eggs. Goldeneyes customarily nest in holes in trees, as do many other species, such as the Goosander (American Merganser) and the Pygmy Goose. Such nesting behavior has permitted different species of waterfowl to breed in the same area with a minimum of conflict over space. ■ Duck nests are well camouflaged. Aided by the dull plumage of the female, they blend into their setting so well that they are invisible to high-flying birds of prey. And a man walking through the area may not dis-

Goldeneye, in tree hole from which its young must drop after they hatch, and Pink-footed Geese, on a steep arctic precipice, exemplify broad range of waterfowl nest sites.

cover a nest until he has nearly stepped on an incubating female. ∎ Drakes rarely stand guard beside their mates during the incubation period. When females leave their nests to feed, they cover the eggs with down or with leaves or grass. On rare occasions when a female returns she sits on the wrong nest, even one of another species if the nests are similar and close by. If such a mistake occurs and the eggs hatch, the foster-mother will rear the strange ducklings as her own. ∎ The eggs of most waterfowl are white, although those of some species may be tinged with blue or green.

In their selection of nest sites and behavior during incubation of the eggs, waterfowl show marked differences. Among most ducks, protection of the nest is accomplished through camouflage. Females, who sit on the nests, have dusky plumage that blends with grassy environs. The drakes do not stay near the nests. But with geese and swans, defense of the nest is the province of aggressive males.

Hawaiian Goose

Canada Goose

Spectacled Eider

European Teal

Red-breasted Merganser

Lesser White-fronted
Goose

Shelduck

Black-necked Swan

Mallard

Greater Scaup

Smew

Black Scoter

Mallard

Pintail

Baikal Teal

Redhead

Canvasback

Bufflehead

Shelduck

Ruddy Duck

Steller's Eider

Geese and swans generally lay clutches of 5 or 6 eggs, except for the Mute Swan, which lays 9 to 11. The nests of ducks sometimes contain as many as 20 eggs, but when the number is that high it usually indicates that more than one female has laid eggs in the same nest. One wild Ruddy Duck is known to have laid 14 eggs within 15 days; they weighed a total of 3 pounds, approximately 3 times the duck's own weight. This was probably a record yield—or very close to it—for any wild species. ■ Almost as soon as they are hatched, the young of waterfowl face danger. Mammals, gulls, and birds of prey snatch them from the nests, and fish attack them when they begin to swim. The danger is greatest for ducklings; ganders and cobs help to protect their young, but drakes do not. In some species of ducks, such as Eiders, separate clutches of ducklings may gather together, and the females watching over them receive some assistance from non-breeding females.

The young of swans, geese, and ducks are covered with down at hatching and they are able to swim as soon as the down is dry. In cases where more than

Some adult ducks, including females, migrate to special areas to molt before the ducklings reach maturity, and only a few females remain on the breeding grounds to do sentry duty. The result is that a large number of ducklings are lost to predators. ■ Because waterfowl do not begin to incubate their eggs until the entire clutch has been laid, all the young in one nest hatch at about the same time. They leave the nest quickly, usually with a little coaxing from the mother. Leaving the nest is difficult for the young of species like the Goldeneyes, which nest in tree holes. The mother flies to the ground, stands beside the tree, and calls up to her ducklings. After much encouragement, the ducklings climb to the rim of the hole and, one at a time, spread their tiny wings and drop perhaps 20 or 30 feet to the ground below. When they are safely on the ground, the mother leads them to water. Young geese that must emerge from nests built on precipitous

one duck species inhabits crowded nesting grounds, eggs from different species may be laid in the same nests, and females incubate and rear foster-progenies.

Great Snow Goose

Canada Goose

Kelp Goose

Hawaiian Goose

Andean Teal

Trumpeter Swan

Ruddy Shelduck

Cape Barren Goose

Emperor Goose

ledges are known to pick their way down the rocks to the sea, but just how they can accomplish this so successfully is still a puzzle to ornithologists. ■ In their first hours of life, young waterfowl learn to recognize their mothers—or mother-substitutes. Goslings have been known to follow the first moving object they see after hatching, and they have attached themselves to humans and other animals. Domesticated ducklings often follow hens, although once they are brought to water they usually jump in and forsake their land-lubberly foster-mothers. ■ Young waterfowl must pick up their own food but are usually guided to it by the females. They are hardy infants who quickly learn to be independent. From the beginning, they are skillful divers. By autumn, the young that have survived predators and the competition for

Ducklings get the bare minimum of parental protection. A female, such as the Mallard shown at left, often watches over a clutch including the abandoned brood of another mother. But goslings, like the young Grey Lags tucked under mother's wing, and cygnets, such as these Black Swan young riding piggyback on a pen, usually know the comforts of watchful care.

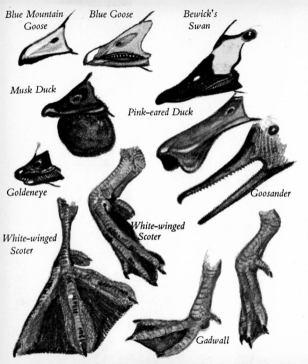

Blue Mountain Goose

Blue Goose

Bewick's Swan

Musk Duck

Pink-eared Duck

Goldeneye

Goosander

White-winged Scoter

White-winged Scoter

Gadwall

Although waterfowl have many traits in common, diverse life opportunities have encouraged evolutionary modifications. Geese, because they eat grasses, have high, pincerlike bills. Goosanders have slim, saw-toothed beaks with which they catch fish. Diving ducks, like the Scoters, usually have large webbings for efficient underwater propulsion.

food have grown flight feathers and are ready to take their places beside the adults in the long migratory flight to the wintering grounds. ■Perhaps the most important influence on the physical evolution of any animal is its food and what it must do to get that food. Most waterfowl, other than geese, feed on aquatic plant and animal life; they must swim, and so they have developed webbed feet as an aid in swimming. They must trap and strain their meals from the water, and so they have wider and flatter bills than birds that live on land. Furthermore, their bills are fitted with comblike teeth that make perfect strainers. ■ Geese, however, graze on land, and they have leg, foot, and bill structures that differ from those of ducks and swans. An example is the long-legged Magpie Goose of Australia, which has only the rudiments of webbing between its toes. For better balance on land, it has a hind toe longer than that of any related bird. The Magpie Goose is so much better adapted for walking than for swimming that it even mates on shore, something that no other wild member of the family Anatidae does. The bills of geese are distinctively higher and stronger than those of ducks, because the geese use them to crop grasses. ∎ Specialization related to diet has produced some oddities among ducks. One of the oddest is the huge, spatula-like bill of the Shoveller, with its fine comblike serra-

The Shoveller gets its name from its spatula-shaped bill that has food strainers on its margins. Young have conventional-shaped bills when they hatch; these change when they are about two weeks old.

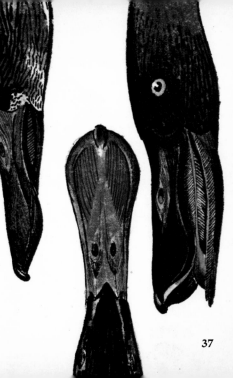

tions. This adaptation permits it to sift the surface of the water for small aquatic insects and plants. ■ The outstanding characteristic of the swan, its long and graceful neck, is a feeding adaptation that allows the bird to reach some 4 or 5 feet below the surface of the water and pick up edible vegetation at the bottom. When a flock of swans is feeding in this manner, at least one acts as sentry, crying out at

Waterfowl have heads and bills that are colorful and varied enough to help in identification. Species shown are: 1. Ruddy Shelduck 2. Snow Goose 3. Canada Goose 4. Radjah Shelduck 5. Lesser White-fronted Goose 6. White-fronted Goose 7. Barnacle Goose 8. Swan Goose 9. Bean Goose 10. Barheaded Goose 11. Green Pygmy Goose 12. Brant 13. Pink-footed Goose 14. Red-breasted Goose 15. Whooper Swan 16. Mute Swan, imm. 17. Mute Swan, ad. 18. Shelduck 19. Bewick's Swan 20. Magpie Goose 21. Egyptian Goose 22. Andean Goose 23. Grey Lag Goose 24. Ruddy-headed Goose 25. Black Swan 26. Hawaiian Goose

any sign of approaching danger. ■ Waterfowl have, generally, benefited from dietary specialization, but it has put some species at a disadvantage. The experience of the American Brant, a favorite of sportsmen, is an example: it has been threatened with extinction in recent years because of its pronounced preference for eelgrass. The flocks customarily spend their winters on the Atlantic coast, where they graze

27. Cape Barren Goose 28. Red-crested Pochard 29. White-winged Scoter 30. Old Squaw 31. King Eider 32. Black Scoter, ♀ 33. Black Scoter, ♂ 34. Eider 35. Spectacled Eider 36. Goosander 37. Red-breasted Merganser 38. Hooded Merganser 39. Tufted Duck 40. Pochard 41. Smew 42. Harlequin 43. Common Goldeneye 44. Barrow's Goldeneye 45. Spur-winged Goose 46. European Widgeon 47. Garganney 48. Rosy-billed Pochard 49. Ferruginous Duck 50. Comb Duck 51. White-backed Duck 52. Magellanic Steamer Duck 53. White-headed Duck 54. Muscovy Duck.

in eelgrass beds at ebb tide. They prefer the enlarged roots and bleached bases of the leaves of eelgrass. It is not uncommon to find masses of this plant, that have been pulled up by these geese, floating on the water. Beginning in 1931, practically all the eelgrass on the Atlantic shore died off, and as a consequence, the Brant population was drastically reduced. Only in the last few years has the eelgrass begun to grow back, and at present the numbers of Brant seem to be increasing. ■ Dabbling ducks, on the other hand, have a diet which gives them a far greater chance for survival. Also known as river and pond ducks, this large group includes such species as Pintails, Mallards, Baldpates, and Widgeons. Pintails have unusually long necks for ducks and enjoy an advantage in bottom-feeding. Their diet, however, is fairly typical of all dabbling ducks, for they also feed in prairie meadows and grain fields remote from water. According to a study of the stomach contents of many specimens, Pintails

Swans, with their long necks, usually feed on submerged plants, while geese, like this Pink-footed flock (right), get their food on land.

eat a variety of foods in the following proportions: pond-weeds, 28%; sedges, 22%; grasses, 10%; smartweeds and docks, 5%; arrow grass, 4%; musk grass and other algae, 3%; arrowhead, water plantain, goosefoot, water lilies, and other miscellaneous plant food, 15%; mollusks, crustaceans, and insects, 13%. With such a varied diet, dabbling ducks have successfully established themselves in all parts of the world; it is unlikely that they will ever suffer a drop in population as sharp as that experienced by the Brants. ■ There are many extremely specialized feeders among the ducks. While all waterfowl have bills with sensitive tips that enable them to feed at night or under water, where they can barely see, one species, the Pink-eared Duck of Australia, has developed two curious soft flaps at the tip of the bill. Feeding is something of a social occasion for this species. Two of the ducks face each other and swim slowly around in a circle. Their bills almost touch beneath the water, which might suggest some form of communication between them involving the use of

Dabbling ducks, like these Pintails, feed by tipping at the surface.

the sensitive bill flaps, although this is not known. ■ The Torrent Ducks of South America also have very soft bills which they slip under the rocks at the bottom of streams to pick up larvae of insects. The Mergansers, with their saw-toothed bills, pursue and catch fish under water. ■ Diving ducks, especially the Eiders, have strong, heavy bills adapted for prying mollusks from stones in the sea; the stomach of one specimen was found to contain 185 mussels. Eiders dive to depths of about 35 or 40 feet to feed. The same depth is reached by the Pochards, a large group of diving ducks with huge, webbed feet and lobed hind toes. Perhaps the best of the divers is the Old Squaw, specimens of which are sometimes taken from fishing nets set at depths of 50 to 180 feet. ■ In an environment dominated by man, the future of the world's waterfowl is uncertain. The Korean Shelduck is known today only from two museum specimens and from Japanese art and literature. The Labrador Duck became extinct as early as 1875, when the last known member of the

The Goosander, largest Merganser, often swims far underwater to catch fish.

species was shot off Long Island. Some species, although protected by law, are threatened with extinction today. They include the magnificent Trumpeter Swan, Ross's Goose, and the Black-bellied Tree Duck. That they can still survive if man practices conservation is shown by the example of the Hawaiian Goose, which was saved from extinction during the past decade. It was bred in captivity and then released into the wild. ■ As the human population rises, life becomes more precarious for waterfowl, and once a species dies out, it cannot be revived. Man himself is the loser, for he has always found enjoyment and refreshment in observing waterfowl. Only man can save them, and preserve for himself the joy of seeing the plumage of ducks, the stately movement of swans, and the swift, free flight of geese across the autumn sky.

Lost to extinction is this lovely Korean Shelduck, known only from ancient Japanese art and some museum skins.

INDEX